Orienteering
Handbook

hancock

house

HANCOCK HOUSE PUBLISHERS

These books have been prepared for the Ministry of Education, Province of British Columbia under the direction of the Secondary Physical Education Curriculum Revision Committee (1980). Members of this committee were:

James Appleby   Gerry Gilmore   Mike McKee
Alex Carr   George Longstaff   Norman Olenick
Madeline Gemmill   John Lowther   David Turkington

ISBN 0-88839-047-5

Canadian Cataloguing in Publication Data

Anthony, Anne.
   Orienteering handbook and curriculum guide
(Physical education series)

   Bibliography: p.
   ISBN 0-88839-047-5 pa.
   1. Orientation - Training. I. Title.
II. Series: Physical Education Series (North
Vancouver, B.C.)
GV200.4.A57   796.4'2'0712   C80-091143-1

Editor Barbara Herringer
Design & Production Paul Willies
Cover Photo Paul Bond
Typeset by Dana Cleland *in Megaron type on an AM Varityper Comp/Edit*

Printed in Canada

Published by
HANCOCK HOUSE PUBLISHERS LTD.
#10 Orwell St. North Vancouver, B.C. V7J 3K1

Table of Contents

Chapter Four

Sample Lesson Plans

Chapter Five

Evaluation

Chapter Six

Making an Orienteering Map

Chapter Seven
Setting an Orienteering Course

Chapter Eight
Organizing an Orienteering Meet

Conclusion
Integration of Orienteering into the Curriculum

Acknowledgments

   I would like to express my sincere thanks to these fellow orienteers for their contribution to this handbook: the late Sass Peepre, University of Guelph, first president of the Canadian Orienteering Federation and founder of Orienteering in Canada.
   Helene Huculak, Executive Director of Silva Ltd., Willowdale, Ontario.
   Jack Lee, Physical Education Consultant, Hamilton Board of Education, Hamilton, Ontario; member of the Education Committee, Canadian Orienteering Federation.
   Jim Gilchrist, Physical Educator, Richmond Hill School District, Toronto, Ontario; member of the Education Committee, Canadian Orienteering Federation.
   Colin Kirk, Executive Director, Canadian Orienteering Federation.
   Members of the Orienteering Association of British Columbia.

Chapter One
Format and Purpose of the Handbook

A. Introduction: *What is Orienteering?*

Orienteering is a forest sport that demands a certain degree of fitness and mental agility. Participants are given a map and compass and once the basic skills of map reading and compass use are developed, they will test their navigational ability around a simple course set out on the school campus or in the local park. They will become more reliant on their powers of observation and decision-making concerning the selection of routes and, as a result, navigational skill and self-confidence will increase. They will be able to enjoy the challenge of a more competitve style of the sport such as a small school event in which they will go cross-country Orienteering. They will travel alone remembering to keep their maps always oriented to north and they will begin to estimate the distance traveled by pace counting. They will locate a sequence of orange and white flags set out in the forest, check the control code before punching their score card and set their course to the next control. They will be aware of the fact that all participants are competing against the clock and that it would be foolish to travel too quickly making unnecessary mistakes. Yet regardless of the time taken, they will experience the exhiliration of crossing the finish line having successfully completed the course. Orienteering is for all levels of expertise and ability and enjoyment is gained from the individual's participation.

The sport of Orientation originated in Scandinavia in the early nineteen twenties, where it began as part of military training. Gradually, a competitive activity developed as the basic equipment of a map and compass became more sophisticated. The term "Orienteering" was coined by the Kjellestrom brothers, and became an international word as the sport spread from Europe to other parts of the world. At the present time Canada is one of 26 Orienteering nations. See Appendix II, Historical Background.

B. Purpose of the Handbook

This handbook is an extension of the Physical Education Curriculum and Resource Guide (1980). The information included in the handbook is designed to provide the instructor with a comprehensive source of information for the teaching of Orienteering.

C. Handbook Format

The teaching of Orienteering should begin with simple activities and progress to the more complex. However, progression is dependent on the individual participant rather than being determined by any Grade level. The levels approach, explained later in this chapter, has been developed to reinforce this concept. The guidelines presented in this handbook are suggestions only and may be adapted as the instructor becomes more familiar with Orienteering.

D. Objectives of the Program

Orienteering is a lifetime sport. It encourages enjoyment and appreciation of activity in a park or forest setting and establishes greater awareness and thoughtful use of the environment. Participants learn decision-making and self-reliance as well as keen observation and attention to detail. An increase in general levels of physical fitness is also developed. Orienteering has been called the 'thinking sport' since the participant is challenged to think while traveling through the forest. The sport gives a sense of success that may be achieved at any level of participation and is an inexpensive activity for all ages - the young or the young at heart.

The Orienteering program has three major objectives:

1. Psychomotor Objectives

    a) Participants should be able to handle the compass correctly.
    b) Participants should learn how to estimate distance by pace counting.
    c) Participants should improve their general level of fitness.
    d) Participants should be able to run over different terrain without difficulty.

2. Cognitive Objectives

    a) Participants should be aware of the historical development of Orienteering.
    b) Participants should acquire map reading skills.
    c) Participants should be able to demonstrate sound navigational skills.
    d) Participants should be able to analyze route choices after a competition.
    e) Participants should be able to understand competitive procedures.

3. Affective Objectives

    a) Participants should develop a positive attitude to the program through enthusiastic involvement.

b) Participants should be encouraged to work independently to develop their own powers of decision-making.

c) Participants should demonstrate responsibility and safety in their independent activity.

E. Application to Classroom Teaching

Orienteering may be taught in a variety of locations depending on the material presented in the lesson. It is suggested that initially a classroom or indoor area would be appropriate, followed by activity progressing from the gymnasium to playing field, school campus and local park. Flexibility in the selection of the most suitable environment is an important consideration in program planning.

However, learning occurs best through activity and any successful experience will develop a positive attitude and enhance the learning potential of the participants.

F. Description of Levels Approach

In a comprehensive Physical Education curriculum, emphasis should be placed on the provision of a sound framework for individual development. One way of doing this is to use a sequentially developed program of physical activities that integrates affective, cognitive and psychomotor areas. This focus is called a "levels" approach.

Orienteering uses a four-level system as follows:

Level I	-	Beginner
Level II	-	Novice
Level III	-	Intermediate
Level IV	-	Advanced

Each level introduces and develops some of the essential skills. The successive levels reinforce the existing skills and introduce new material in sequence. This process allows the basic skills and practical application to become thoroughly developed in a variety of situations.

G. Explanation of Activity Sequence Chart

The Activity Sequence Chart outlines a progressive pattern of skills that are required for Orienteering. The chart serves as a sequence guide in planning sessions and indicates the level at which each skill should be introduced. As learning continues, a skill is reinforced and built upon. For example, "Orienting the Map" is introduced as a Level I skill and subsequent activities with the map will reinforce this skill at other levels.

The instructor may refer to Chapters Two and Four for further assistance and more detailed information.

H. Activity Sequence Chart

SKILLS   LEVELS

Skill	I	II	III	IV
A. Introduction				
1. Definitions of the sport	•			
2. Historical development	•			
3. Running techniques-map oriented	•			
B. Map				
1. Types of maps	•			
2. Map Characteristics	•			
3. Orienting the map	•			
4. Recognition of map symbols	•			
5. Feature identification	•			
6. Relationship between map and terrain	•			
7. Contour interval	•			
8. Map reading by thumb	•			
9. Map memory		•		
10. Rough map reading		•		
11. Magnetic declination				•
12. Precision map reading				•
C. Compass				
1. Identification of parts	•			
2. Function of each part	•			
3. Holding compass	•			
4. Define magnetic north	•			
5. Identify compass points	•			
6. Taking a compass bearing	•			
7. Facing a bearing	•			
8. Orienting by needle	•			
9. Combining pacing and following compass bearing		•		
10. Rough compass		•		
11. Precision compass			•	
12. Back bearings				•
D. Map and Compass				
1. Taking compass bearing from map		•		
E. Estimation of Distance				
1. Pacing over measured distance: walk	•			
jog		•		
run			•	
2. Measuring by eye	•			
3. Pacing across different terrains		•		
4. Pacing over varying distance		•		

SKILLS	I	II	III	IV
5. Distance judgment on map using compass scale		●		
6. Contour interval		●		
7. Relationship between vertical height and horizontal distance			●	
F. Navigation				
1. Fundamental guidelines:				
use of open area	●			
use of trails	●			
use of large features	●			
2. Route selection:				
direct	●			
alternative	●			
3. Navigational techniques:				
attack point		●		
aiming off		●		
collecting feature		●		
handrails		●		
4. Control simplification		●		
5. Control locations - numbered on circles on map	●			
6. Independent navigation	●			
7. Mentally walk to first control	●			
8. Contouring		●		
9. Traffic light navigation			●	
G. Competitive Techniques				
1. Recognition of control flag	●			
2. Master map	●			
3. Control description sheet	●			
4. Start and finish symbols	●			
5. Pre-marked map	●			
6. Time interval	●			
7. Safety bearings	●			
8. Map case - folded map		●		
H. Types of Competition				
1. Miniature	●			
2. Distance and Direction	●			
3. Score	●			
4. Line		●		
5. Team / Relay		●		
6. Cross-Country			●	
7. Night				●
8. Mountain Marathon				●
I. Map Making				
1. Types of maps	●			

SKILLS	I	II	III	IV
2. Drawing simple maps	●			
J. Course Setting				
1. Setting simple course on school campus or local park		●		

I. Relationship of Orienteering to Goals and Learning Outcomes

Active participation in an Orienteering program should realize the following goals:

1. Participants should demonstrate a greater degree of fitness and increase their running capability through different terrains and at greater speeds.

2. Participants should demonstrate efficient use of the compass, be able to pace count, and perform navigational skills while traveling outdoors.

3. Participants should demonstrate an understanding of map reading skills, the role of the compass, navigational techniques and basic competitive procedures.

4. Participants should demonstrate a positive attitude towards their level of expertise, to develop individual powers of decision-making, and to value participation in Orienteering as a life time activity.

Chapter Two
Skill Development: Techniques And Definitions

The material presented in this chapter follows the Activity Sequence Chart which is outlined in Chapter One. The right-hand column provides either the definition and/or teaching technique for the skills or characteristics listed in the left-hand column. All major headings in this chapter are expanded upon in both Chapters Three and Four.

A. The Map

Definition: A picture of the ground.

1. Types of Maps
a) topographical
b) Orienteering
c) street
d) campus

Different maps may be used during the unit. Maps establish the relationship of ground to maps and assist in the identification of specific locations.

2. Characteristics of Maps
a) Colors
   i) brown
   ii) black
   iii) blue
   iv) yellow
   v) green

-Represents contours and relief features
-Represents man-made features
-Represents water systems
-Represents open area
-Represents vegetation features

b) Color aids to navigation

Blue and green would be areas to avoid, as they represent water and dense forest. Yellow and black would be easy navigation across an open area or along a trail.

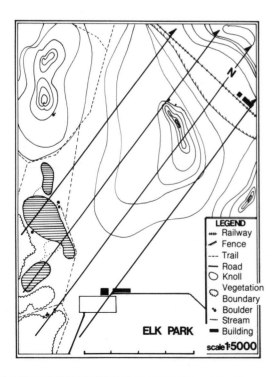

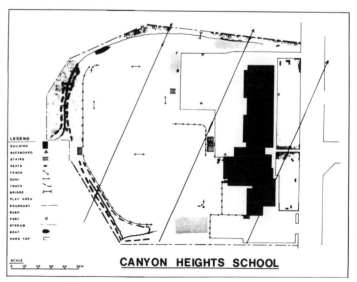

c) Contours:

Lines drawn on the map which join points of the same elevation.
Contour lines that are close together denote steepness; those widely spaced show a gradual slope.

d) Legend:

Identifies all features, however small, that appear on the map. Even a one meter boulder will be represented by a small black dot.

e) Scale:

The ratio of the distance on the map to the distance on the ground. Refers to the amount of terrain represented by each centimeter on the map. A map scale of 1:10,000 cm. can be translated to one cm. on the map representing 10,000 cm. or 100 m. on the ground.

f) Magnetic North:

Magnetic compasses are used in Orienteering. Maps are drawn to Magnetic North in order to correspond with the compass. Magnetic North is illustrated by arrowheads at the top of each meridian line.

3. Orienting the Map

This is an important aspect of Orienteering. The map should always be oriented to north by matching Magnetic North (lines) on the map to the direction of Magnetic North on the ground (by use of compass). The direction of travel is then determined correctly.

4. Recognition of Map Symbols

Each feature on the map has an equivalent symbol representation in the legend. These symbols have to be readily recognized to assist in map reading.

5. Feature Identification

This aspect of map reading relates to the recognition of map symbols. It is important to travel in the forest and learn to make the relationship between feature and symbol.

6. Relationship Between Map and Terrain

Participants learn to know where they are on the map and on the terrain simultaneously, matching their exact location visually.

7. Contour Interval

The contour interval, generally five meters is always stated on the map.

8. Map Reading by Thumb

This is a simple, yet important, technique.
The participant's location is identified by placing the thumb on the map to mark the last exact known location. The thumb is moved to different locations on the map as the participant travels the route.

9. Map Memory

An advanced technique in which the participant attempts to memorize the particular section of the map that has been chosen as a route to the next control. This technique allows the participant to travel with greater speed.

10. Rough Map Reading

A more advanced navigational technique that allows the participant to travel fairly quickly through an area while making only general references to the map.

11. Magnetic Declination

Magnetic declination is the difference between true north and magnetic north. The magnetic declination from true north is 23° east for the Vancouver area and 15° west in Ottawa. Contact local association for specific magnetic declinations for various areas.

12. Precision Map Readings

The participant travels carefully in a straight line from one feature to the next with constant reference to the map.

B. The Compass

Definition: The compass gives direction.

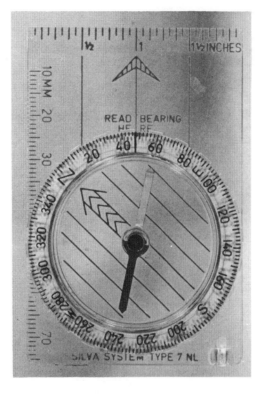

direction of travel arrow

north arrow (striped)

base plate

compass housing   magnetic needle (red)

1. Identification of Parts

a) base plate   -Flat rectangular surface
b) housing   -Circular rotating section
c) magnetic needle   -Red needle
d) north arrow   -Striped red arrow
e) direction of travel arrow   -Black arrow at the front of the compass

2. Function of Compass Parts
   a) base plate — Part of compass that is held in the hand.
   b) housing — Gives identification of compass bearing.
   c) magnetic needle — Always points to Magnetic North.
   d) north arrows — Used in conjunction with map to determine direction of travel.
   e) direction of travel arrow — Direction in which to travel (nose of the compass).

3. Holding the Compass

   Initially the compass should be held between first fingers and thumbs and at waist level. The direction of travel arrow points in front (nose leads the way). A cord is normally attached to the compass and secured to the wrist and the compass is carried on one hand at waist level.

4. Define Magnetic North

   Magnetic needle and north arrow are aligned. The participant is then oriented to Magnetic North.

5. Identification of Compass

   Points of the compass are North, South, East and West.

6. Taking a Compass Bearing

   a) Point compass in general direction of travel.
   b) Rotate compass housing until (red) magnetic needle is aligned directly over the (striped) north arrow.
   c) Read bearing at the base of the direction of travel arrow.
   d) Follow the direction of travel arrow.

7. Orienting by Needle

   Compass can be oriented when north arrow is directly aligned with the magnetic needle.

8. Facing a Bearing

   Set compass and identify feature in direct path of travel.

9. Combination of Pacing and Following a Compass Bearing

   Count the number of paces along a given compass bearing.

10. Rough Compass

   Follow in the general direction, for example, traveling south instead of specifically 176°, the participant checks only that the red magnitic needle is aligned with the striped north arrow.

11. Precision Compass

   Precise compass bearings are taken from feature to feature so participant travels in a straight line.

12. Back Bearings

   Align the white end of the magnetic needle with the north arrow and return to last known feature location in order to become re-oriented.

C. Map and Compass

Taking Compass
Bearing from
Map

An advanced technique. Use the three-stage method:
a) Place the long edge of the compass on map linking the point of departure to the intended destination.
b) Rotate the compass housing so that the lines are parallel with the meridian lines on the map. The north arrow on the compass should also be pointing to the arrowheads at the top of each meridian line.
c) Take the compass off the map. Hold it in the prescribed manner at waist level. Become oriented by turning body, map and compass so that magnetic needle is over north arrow. Read bearing. This is the direction in which to travel.

D. Estimation of Distance

1. Pacing Over
   Measured
   Distance

Set up traffic cones a specific distance apart and have participants walk, jog, and run over the distance, counting alternate strides. Two walking strides are equal to one Orienteering pace.

2. Measuring By Eye

Visually judge distance from present location to destination, then check out accuracy of estimation.

3. Pacing Across
   Different Terrains

Repeat the three styles of travel (walk, jog, run) over rough ground, soft areas and uphill.

4. Pacing Over Varying Distance	Vary length of pacing along trails and across open areas.
5. Distance Judgment on Map	Estimation of distance between two points on the map using compass.
6. Contour Interval	Contour lines give approximate distance.
7. Relationship of Vertical and Horizontal Distance	Understanding of contours in a three dimensional manner.

E. Navigation

Use of an Orienteering map is important.

1. Fundamental Guidelines

a) Use a trail, if there is one in the general area.
b) Keep to open areas for faster and easier navigation.
c) Travel around large features such as a lake, so that exact location on map is known.

TRAIL	OPEN AREA	LARGE FEATURE
a)	b)	c)

2. Route Selection

A trail
B contouring
C over the hill

a) Direct Route

-Taking the most direct route regardless of the terrain. This is best done over short distances and when nearing the control location.

b) Alternative Route

-Choice of route that allows the participant to make the best use of the terrain and yet still maintain reasonable speed.

3. Navigational Techniques

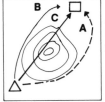

a) Attack Point

-A large feature that is located between the participant and the control, hence reducing the margin of error in locating the control

b) Aiming Off

-Compass bearing is taken so that the participant arrives to one side of the control. Most effective with a linear feature such as a stream.

c) Collecting Feature

-Generally, a linear feature that is located directly behind the control, thus preventing the participant from going on too far past the control location.

d) Handrail

-A large feature, such as a lake, that the participant runs beside without constant reference to map or compass.

4. Control	A large feature on which an orange and white tubular flag has been placed. The participant navigates to this location.

5. Control Locations	Recognition of feature(s) identified by the circle on the map.
6. Control Simplification	Some control locations are small features on or near a larger feature. Endeavor to find this feature fist to assist navigation.
7. Independent Navigation	Individual participation is the nature of Orienteering.
8. Mentally Walk to First Control	Participant *must* be aware of the relationship of map and terrain from the Start location.
9. Contouring	Participant runs at same elevation to avoid traveling up and down unnecessarily.
10. "Traffic Light" Navigation	An advanced and sensible technique. When nearing the control location the participant slows from a run to a jog to reduce the risk of errors.

F. Competitive Techniques

Have the equipment available as necessary.

1. Recognition of Control Flag	Orange and white nylon tubular flag.
a) Control Code	-Numbers (or letters) which identify each control flag.

| | b) Control Punch | -Orange stapler that leaves a distinctive imprint on the control card. It is attached to the flag. |

2. Master Map

Map on which the course is printed. The participants copy the course on their own maps from the Master Map.

3. Control Description Sheet

A sheet attached to the map that gives information about features (control locations) to be found during the event.

	YELLOW 2·6 km		
Control Number	**(Control Feature)**	**Control Code**	**(Control Symbol)**
1	Trail, junction	AB	
2	Fence, east corner	RS	
3	Marsh, north edge	VE	
4	Stream, path, intersection	TJ	X
5	Boulder	LD	1M

4. Control Card

Participant marks this card in some way as evidence of locating each control.

5. Start and Finish Symbols

Triangle represents the Start. Double circle is the Finish symbol.

6. Pre-marked Map

Course has been printed on map before start of event.

7. Time Interval

Time allowed between the start of each participant.

8. Safety Bearing

A bearing (for example, 33°) may be printed on the map that will lead the participant to a road or large feature close to the Start/Finish area.

9. Map Case

Gives protection from the weather.

Chapter Three
Activities, Games And Events

A. Fitness

The current interest in jogging, cycling and other outdoor pursuits should encourage participants to exercise regularly on their own. A simple fitness program that combines running and technique training is invaluable for the Orienteering program since it encourages activity as well as generating interest in the sport.

1. Running Activities

Easy jog for 15-20 minutes several times each week. Jog in Orienteering terrain, for instance in a hilly area or over uneven ground.

2. Technique Training

Running is the basis of Orienteering. In order to relieve the possible monotony of jogging, various navigational games may be played.

a) Follow the Leader:
   Leader selects a point on the map and travels there. The group follows and describes the exact route traveled.
b) Map Memory:
   With a partner, select a point on the map and memorize its location before traveling to that same point. On arrival, partner with the map checks the accuracy of route taken.
c) Relay Run:
   Two controls are placed in the park and each group member has to locate them in turn.

B. Activities And Games

These activities and games will introduce and reinforce basic Orienteering skills. By becoming more familiar with map and compass procedures in a game situation, participants will be able to progress to more challenging outdoor events.

*Indicates that these games are available from Canadian Orienteering Services (Silva Ltd.). See Appendix I for address.

1. Map Games

a) Map Symbol Relay Game
   The purpose of this game is to test map symbol identification skills. The cards used have a map symbol on one side and a written description on the other. These do not correspond.

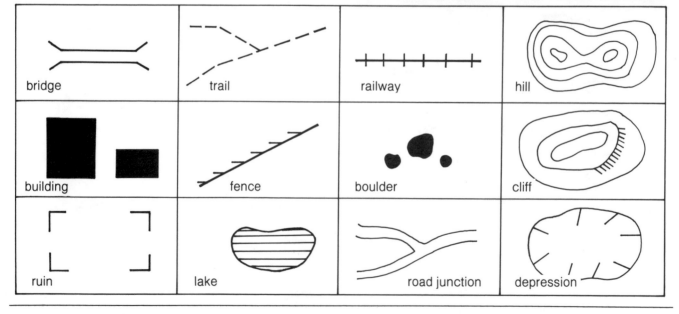

bridge	trail	railway	hill
building	fence	boulder	cliff
ruin	lake	road junction	depression

Divide participants into four groups. Spread one set of symbols face-up on the floor at a suitable distance in front of each group. Give each leader a symbol card (start card). All leaders receive the same symbol.

When the participants receive their start cards, for example, with the map symbol "stream," they turn them over to find that they must identify "railway," as printed on the card. They run to the area where the symbol cards are located, find the card illustrating "railway," place their start cards (face-up) with the rest of the cards and return the new card illustrating railway to the person next in line. This is continued until the symbol "stream" (or the start card) has been identified.

b) Map Memory Relay Game

The purpose of this game is to encourage quick and accurate identification of features, and to appreciate the relationship between the circled location and another easily recognized feature in order to successfully remember the exact location.

Divide participants into groups. Give each group a map and red pencil. At some distance away place a master map on which a course with the △ and ⊙ representing the Start and Finish, as well as nine circled control locations have been marked.

The first group member must run to the master map, identify the exact circle location of the first control (beginning with the Start symbol) then quickly return to the group map and carefully record the information. When the participant puts the pencil down, the next member runs to the master map to locate the next control.

The game continues until each group has reproduced the entire course onto their own map. Before doing a comparison with the master map, the group must write the control descriptions on the map and number each of the circle locations in sequence, including the Start and Finish.

It is suggested that after the more active part of the game, the participants discuss the possible routes that each could have taken around the course. This is the most worthwhile aspect of the activity since it reinforces basic navigational and map reading skills.

c) Try Map Reading

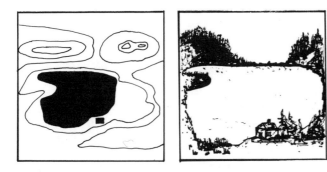

Design a sheet which consists of a section of an Orienteering map in the center and six to eight pictures of locations. The pictures are numbered, locations on the map are lettered. Participants must match numbers to the letters to obtain the correct map location to the picture. This activity encourages use of basic map reading skills.

d) Orienting the Map

The most important aspect of Orienteering is that the map be oriented at all times. The arrrow indicating North on the map should point to North so that map and terrain are correctly aligned. The direction of travel is determined by the way the map is held.

Design a sheet that has four pictures. Under each there are four map drawings, but only one is correctly oriented to the picture. Match up the corresponding map drawings and pictures.

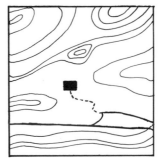

e) Map Memory and Verbal Navigation

Divide participants into groups of four and give each group the same map. The first participant from each group goes to a master map on which two features are circled. They must memorize the exact location of the features before returning to the goup. Without being able to touch or indicate on the map, they must verbally navigate their group from the first feature to the second location. When this has been successfully completed, the next member of the group identifies the two features on the master map, and if correct, is given two different feature locations. The game is repeated until every member of the group has had a turn. (The group that does this activity in the shortest time is deemed to have the best verbal navigators!)

f) Follow John or Jane

This navigational game demands careful observation of the terrain and features that the participants are traveling past while following the leader. In other words, the participants are attempting visual map reading while running. This activity is for those who have map reading experience and enjoy the challenge of being able to record mentally, through careful observation, the route taken between different locations.

Divide participants into groups of four or five. Each person must have a map, but only the leader will be able to look at it. The remaining members of the group must put their maps out of sight, preferably into a pocket.

The leader sets off at a jogging pace. The rest of the group is well spaced out to assist observation and carefully follows the exact route taken by the leader. The leader will stop at a prominent feature and ask the group to identify where they are on the map and show the exact route they took to reach their present location.

There are several variations to this activity. Leadership can be changed so that each member has an opportunity to lead the group. Distances can vary as memory and concentration improve.

g) Chalkboard Orienteering

This activity introduces the relationship between the map and the ground in a familiar environment such as a classroom or gymnasium.

Draw an accurate diagramatic map on the board ensuring that any symbols for chairs, traffic cones, and so forth that may be used on the map, are also included in the legend for easy recognition by the participants.

Set the course by placing small red circular stickers on selected objects. Print a letter on each sticker so that the combined letters make up a short Orienteering phrase.

The exact location of the red stickers should be carefully marked by a circle on the board and numbered (the center of the circle being the actual location of the sticker).

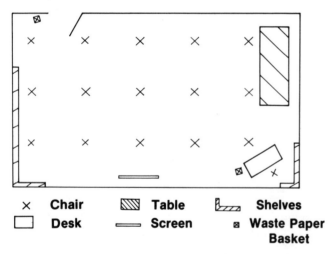

| × | **Chair** | ▨ | **Table** | � | **Shelves** |
| ☐ | **Desk** | ▭ | **Screen** | ⊠ | **Waste Paper Basket** |

The aim of the game is for the participants to locate all the stickers and record the letter beside each number on their score card as quickly as possible, then unscramble the letters into a phrase or sentence. For example, if 17 stickers are placed out the letters could well read "Orienteering is fun."

2. Compass Games

a) Compass Walk on Paper

Take an imaginary walk on graph paper using compass directions. One step is equivalent to one square. The result will be a diagram, for example, a familiar object. This activity makes participants aware of compass directions and reinforces that North is at the top of the page.

b) Indoor Compass Game

In the center of the gym floor, write with chalk as many numbers as there are participants in the class, then tape corresponding numbered cards on all four walls. Give each participant a compass, paper and pencil. Instruct them to find the bearing from the number they are standing on, to the corresponding number on the wall. Each participant must move ahead one number on the floor and record that new bearing to the matching number. Keep playing until participants understand concepts.

*c) Outdoor Compass Game

This activity requires careful use of the compass and consistent pace counting.

Measure out a distance of 150 meters (100 feet). Place twenty markers 1.5 meters (five feet) apart on a straight East-West line. Number markers 1-20. Design twenty separate routes, each having three directions of travel.

Start each of the participants at their own starting marker. They follow the route on their instruction card that gives them three changes of direction and distance before returning them to the line of markers. Have participants repeat this procedure, taking a different course several times. The object of the game is to get as close as possible to the correct finishing marker each time.

d) Hunt the Silver Dollar

This simple indoor or outdoor game gives beginners practise in compass reading and pace counting.

Spread the participants in "scatter formation" in an open area. Have them place a small object between their feet to determine start location.

1. Set the compass at any bearing and orient it to north.
2. Walk a specified number of Orienteering paces in that direction.
3. Add 120° to the original compass bearing and re-set the compass.
4. Walk the same number of paces as before on the new compass bearing.
5. Repeat these two procedures for the third time.

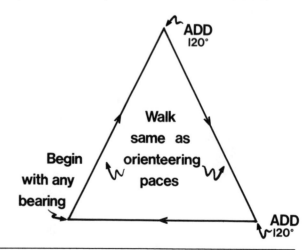

If the directions are followed precisely, each student will have walked in a triangular formation. This activity should be repeated several times using a different initial compass bearing to return them to the object.

Difficulty of the activity can be increased by:

1. Increasing the length of the sides of the figure to be traced.
2. Changing the bearing by a different factor of 360° to trace a different shape; for example, 90° to produce a square, 80° to produce a hexagon.

*e) Schoolyard Compass Game

This game offers a challenging introduction to proper compass usage. It is easy to set up in a small area and requires minimum equipment.

Place a stake in the center of an area and attach a 50 meter measuring tape. Working from the center, place other stakes at varying locations using predetermined compass bearings. Each of the stakes has a letter code.

All participants receive an instruction card that gives their starting position and the bearings which will direct them around their course. Participants start from labeled markers and use compass bearings to move from one marker to another noting the code letters. When all code letters are collected, these are checked with the master sheet. No two instruction cards need be the same.

f) Card Compass Game

Using two sets of identically numbered small cards, place the first set on fifteen locations and the other set on traffic cones in a central location. When standing in front of the number seven traffic cone, for example, the corresponding card seven can be seen at the fence corner.

In partners and with compass, two score cards and pencil, one participant will take compass bearing from in front of each traffic cone to the appropriate feature; the other student will record, on the score card, the direction given by the bearing. Partners will change over and the compass bearings will be taken from the feature to the traffic cone. This information will be recorded on the second score card.

When course has been completed, have students compare results. Hopefully they will find that the second set of compass bearings will be exactly half of the first set!.

This activity can be set up either in the gymnasium or on the playing field.

3. Map and Compass Games

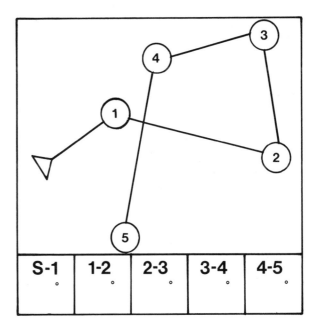

S-1	1-2	2-3	3-4	4-5
°	°	°	°	°

Distance and Direction Activity:

Each participant is given a "blank" map on which only the meridian north lines and the course are printed.

a) Orient the map by turning it so that the triangle that denotes the Start is closest to the participant.
b) Place the compass on the map so that the long edge of the compass links the point of departure (the triangle) to the intended destination (control location #1).
c) Rotate the compass housing, so that the North lines of the compass are pointing to the top or North on the map.
d) Take the compass off the map. Hold it in the prescribed way, that is, at waist level in one hand. Participants must orient themselves by turning around until the red magnetic compass needle is matched directly over the striped north arrow. Then read the bearing - this is the direction in which to travel.

C. Types Of Events

1. Miniature Orienteering

This activity can be organized without too much difficulty or time. All that is needed is a large open space such as a gymnasium, playing field or local park. This game gives participants the "feel" of Orienteering in a familiar environment.

Divide participants into partners and give each pair a compass, small white card and pen. Have the partners carefully copy down and number the list of features (control descriptions). If there are 30 people in the group, 15 different features will be needed.

Each pair must select one of these 15 features as a starting point and go to that chosen location. On arrival they must draw a triangle around the starting number (the triangle is the international symbol for the start of a competition) on their score card.

The aim of this activity is to determine the distance in paces (two walking strides are equal to one Orienteering pace) between the 15 features and to make accurate compass bearings from one feature to the next on the list. This is repeated until each pair has returned to its original starting point.

The distance in paces may be converted into meters and the partners who complete the course first can calculate how far everyone traveled.

The directions should be checked to determine whether accurate compass bearings were taken.

This activity is more meaningful if the distances between features vary in length (the course can be walked and/or jogged).

The course, that is, identifying the features, should be checked ahead of time. One important point to remember is that each feature should be clearly visible from the next feature because the course is continuous.

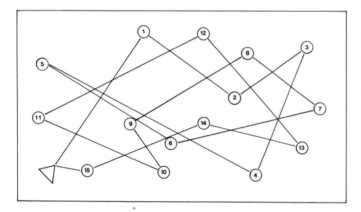

2. Distance and Direction Orienteering

The purpose of this activity is to set a compass carefully and reach a predetermined destination by traveling in a straight line, then to calculate the distance by accurate pace counting.

A course has to be set ahead of time for this activity

but all that is needed is a compass, a set of white cards (14 cm x 20 cm) and a red felt pen.

Select a starting point, such as a fence corner just outside the gymnasium. Now locate another feature within visual distance and take a compass bearing to it. Always take the compass bearing at the same distance from the control; it is important to be consistent around the entire course. Next, pace count to the new feature by traveling in a straight line. Calculate the distance in meters. Record on the card a) the control card number in top left-hand corner, b) distance in meters, c) direction in degrees. Place the card next to the original feature which served as the course starting point. Set the course with care. Accuracy is very important otherwise the participant may unintentionally head in the wrong direction. Attempt to vary the distance (from 100 m to 15 m) between the feature locations.

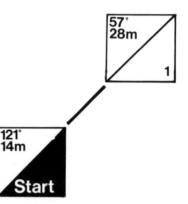

The information on the last control card should lead participants back to the starting point. Control cards should be placed on the far side of the feature away from the approaching participants so they are aiming for the feature and not the card.

To make sure that everyone has been around the course, it is sometimes fun to have a letter code on each card. These letters are recorded as participants travel the course and are then unscrambled into an Orienteering word or phrase.

This activity can be organized on a campus, in school or in the local park. Divide the class into pairs. If the group is particularly large, set two courses in a figure-eight formation with the Start and Finish in the center of the two loops. This will ensure that all participants have enough time to complete the course, and are well spaced out since the two groups will be setting off simultaneously but in different directions.

3. "Do-It-Yourself" Orienteering

An ideal conclusion to any unit is Do-It-Yourself Orienteering because participants are able to work at their own ability level within a set time limit. Careful pre-planning is essential. An Orienteering map of the school campus or local park should be drawn. A course of approximately 15 controls is set in a "scatter formation". Location of these 15 features can be marked with either a regular control flag or a small red sticker. Some form of code letter is required on each control.

The maps should be pre-marked with the circled control locations and each should have a number which is outside the circle. Type up a control descripton sheet; for example, No. 7, fence, northeast corner (P). Prepare another set of 20 maps with only one numbered circle and the control description marked on each.

Divide the group into pairs. Give each pair one map marked with a single control location. Allow some time for participants to study the map, so that they know exactly where to place the control. Send the participants out to set the course. Collect these maps and in exchange distribute the master maps and a score card to each pair.

A variation of this activity is to allow participants to set their own course. Each pair is given a blank map from which they select a possible control location before leaving the classroom. They locate this feature and place the control flag card or small red sticker at the location, then mark the exact location on the map by means of a small circle.

This information is then shared with the group so that before the competition begins, participants will have all feature locations circled and identified on their own maps.

Send the participants to visit all the other control locations within a set time limit and have them record the code letter on the score card.

On returning, each pair must unscramble the code letters into an Orienteering term or phrase: for instance, "the thinking sport." At the end of the activity, students collect the control cards they initially placed out in the schoolyard or park.

4. Score Orienteering

The object in Score Orienteering is to gather, during a specified time limit, as many points as possible by visiting as many control locations as possible. Set the course in a "scatter formation" throughout the area. More controls than can be visited during the time limit should be set up. Each control has a specified point value: controls near the Start-Finish area have a low point value; those farther away or difficult to reach have a high point value.

All participants carry a control description sheet and a map. The map locates each control by number. The description sheet describes the control site location and the control point value. Each control flag has an identifying mark or letter that must be copied by the participants to show that they have visited that particular location.

This type of Orienteering event can be started anywhere there is enough space to keep participants active for fifteen minutes. A school campus or park can be used in the beginning. All that is needed is a well-planned course on a simple black and white map that indicates the main identifiable features so that the participants can orient their maps. With such restrictions of time and space, a Score competition can be run comfortably within an hour.

5. Line Orienteering

Line Orienteering is useful to test both map reading skills and the ability to follow accurately a compass bearing. This activity should be introduced in a familiar area. All participants are given maps with no additional markings on them and must start off at time intervals. After starting, participants visit a master map where they copy a route onto their own map. No control locations are given and the challenge is to follow the exact route copied from the master map.

Control flags will be located randomly along the route. Participants mark the location of these controls accurately on their own maps and note the identifying code marks for each control. Sound map reading skills are necessary to do well in this activity.

6. Relay and Team Orienteering

Orienteering can be made more interesting by having group events. The purpose of this activity is for one group to gain the most points. Groups might range from two to six in number depending on the number of controls set and the size of the area in use. A group leader may assign individuals, partners, or the entire group to visit specific controls.

Novice participants sometimes lack the self-confidence needed for individual line or cross-country Orienteering; this can usually be overcome by participating in pairs, although individual competition is more desirable.

Relay competitions are an interesting variation and can be run in a number of ways. Relays can be organized where participants wait for the return of their group members before starting. Alternatively, each member may leave simultaneously but return to start on a different route. When all group members have returned, the total elapse time and points are calculated.

7. Cross-Country Orienteering

This is Orienteering in its pure form; other types are derived from it. Best performances are decided strictly on a time basis provided the students complete the course properly. Participants are started at time intervals after which they are given either a pre-marked map with their course printed in red, or they follow a well-marked route (usually marked with brightly colored streamers) to a master map area where the location of the control points are copied onto a map. The participant must visit each of the control locations in the specified order. Each control is identified by a code symbol corresponding to the code on the participant's control description sheet. The description sheet is stapled to the map.

This type of event may take more than an hour to complete, so a full morning or afternoon is necessary. Accurate maps are important and the event area should be of uneven terrain and partially wooded with identifiable physical features.

D. Activity Variations

The teaching of Orienteering is not limited to the school campus or local park. It is an activity that can be taught at any time during the year; therefore with sensible organization, Orienteering can be experienced in several different ways:

1. Bicycle Orienteering

A local street map is convenient but when using it always avoid main streets and highways. Select an area within reasonable distance of the school and one which has distinct boundaries, for example, a highway which the participants may not cross. Do not emphasize speed, but encourage accuracy of observation and understanding of directions.

2. Canoe Orienteering

The selection of a lake is secondary to the participants' knowledge of safe and efficient canoeing. All participants should be swimmers and wear life jackets. Canoe Orienteering is most successful as a Score event. See page 23. A novel method for this event is to place a master map on a nearby off-shore island so that participants must paddle to that location in order to receive their map and instructions. Alternatively, have participants stand in pairs behind a Start line. At a given time interval, maps and instructions are picked up before a short sprint to the canoes.

3. Snow Orienteering

There are two factors to consider when setting an Orienteering course in the snow:

a) Since snow levels vary (sometimes hourly) contour lines and features are often drastically altered.
b) A successful event depends upon the participants' level of expertise on cross-country skis or snowshoes.

Line, Score, or Team Orienteering may be adapted for snow events. Keep the course simple! It is advisable when traveling through snow to use a map that has been printed on colored paper. Place maps in ziplock plastic bags and have participants pin them to their jackets. No compasses are used since hands will be holding ski poles. Try to avoid excessive waiting at the Start. If the area is familiar then use map memory, whereby a section of the map has been placed at each control and has been memorized correctly in order to reach the next control.

Chapter Four
Sample Lesson Plans

A. Introduction

Orienteering is an activity that lends itself to the levels approach and within each of the following sample lesson plans it will become clear that participants are developing and progressing at different levels.

The Orienteering activities and game situations make it simpler to instruct participants of varying skill levels since they are learning and performing *individually*. It should be relatively easy therefore, for the instructor to work with Level II and Level III participants simultaneously and to adopt the levels approach with each lesson by offering situations in which all participants may progress at their own levels.

Those who are most fit or who have grasped the basic skills will obviously progress more quickly.

Note that these lesson plans are designed to give a general feel of an orienteering unit, but need not be followed exactly as suggested in this chapter.

It is hoped that instructors will have had an opportunity to participate in an Orienteering event prior to teaching in order to bring greater understanding and personal experience to the unit.

Facilities that may be used in the program are:

- classroom   - school campus
- gymnasium   - local park

This unit of eight lessons has been designed for a class of 30.

Time allotment for each lesson is 50 minutes, with perhaps one field trip.

The following equipment will be needed in the program:

1. 30 copies of school campus and local park maps
2. 30 compasses; one large demonstration compass
3. Small white score cards
4. Orange and white controls, cards or orange stickers
5. Stop watch
6. Pencils
7. A.V. resources
8. Handout material

B. Footwear and Clothing

Normal footwear and clothing for school events should include a pair of sturdy, thick-soled running shoes, knee-length socks, shorts and a T-shirt. For cross-country events, participants should have arms and legs covered to give necessary protection when traveling through the bush.

C. Teaching Materials

Further Orienteering teaching materials are available from Provincial or State associations or from Silva Ltd. See appendix for addresses.

Instructor's Note:

All activity ideas suggested in these lesson plans are explained in the previous chapter.

Lesson One

This first session presents an overview of Orienteering by introducing the basic concepts and skills involved.

Objectives: To introduce the sport of Orienteering.
To understand the function of a map.
To introduce basic map characteristics.

1. Introduction

a) *View film:* For example, "What Makes Them Run?" (See References, Appendix I) If a film is not available, the following topics may be used.

b) Discussion:
   i) Brief historical development
   ii) Basic concepts of the sport
   iii) Importance of map reading and compass skills
   iv) Equipment and clothing
   v) Variations in activity
   vi) Level of fitness

c) Activity:
   Chalkboard Orienteering, which introduces the relationship between a map and the ground, is an ideal game to initiate interest among the participants. See page 20.

2. Development

a) Distribute Orienteering maps.

b) Identify the five map characteristics and their functions:
   i) Color - defines areas for easy-to-difficult navigation.
   ii) Contours - denote a change in elevation.
   iii) Legend - describes the symbols that identify all features.
   iv) Scale - represents the amount of ground as shown on the map.
   v) Magnetic North - all Orienteering maps are drawn to Magnetic North which is indicated at the top of the map.

3. Concluding Activity

Working with a partner: Select two features on the map and describe route taken to reach the destination. Clearly determine the features along the route. Identifying each feature by means of a finger is a way of introducing the concept of "map reading by thumb."

4. Review

Briefly discuss the importance and function of maps to the sport of Orienteering.

Lesson Two

Objectives: To introduce the purpose of the compass.
To introduce the use of the compass.

1. Introduction

a) Brief review of basic concepts of Orienteering.

b) Introduce and discuss the compass and its function by showing a variety of compasses.

2. Development

Distribute compasses to participants.

Instructor's Note:

It would be advisable to use the large demonstration compass during this phase of the lesson.

a) Introduce the parts and functions of the compass:
   i) Base plate
   ii) Compass housing and north lines
   iii) North arrow
   iv) Magnetic needle
   v) Direction of travel arrow

b) Encourage participants to handle the compass so they become familiar with its various parts.

c) Introduce the purpose of the compass - compass gives direction.

3. Activities

a) Correct Method of Holding the Compass
The compass initially should be held close to the stomach and between first fingers and thumb so that the direction of travel arrow (or the nose of the compass) is in front. This will ensure that the participant always will be directly behind the compass. Later the compass will be held in one hand and at waist level.

b) Orienting the Compass
The relationship between the participant and North, or being oriented to North, should be established. First, line up the North arrow (striped) with the direction of travel arrow on the compass. The participant should orient by turning self and compass until the magnetic needle (red) is aligned with the other two arrows. Now, the participant is correctly oriented to North.

c) Taking a Compass Bearing
A simple three-stage method should be followed. Hold the compass in the prescribed manner.

1. Point compass in general direction of travel.
2. Rotate the compass housing so magnetic needle(red) is aligned over the north arrow (striped).
3. Read the bearing at the base of the direction of travel arrow.

Repeat the same procedure several times by giving the participants an opportunity to select various objects (or features) around them.

d) 'Dial' a Compass Bearing
Ask a participant to call out any number smaller than 360° (for instance 97°). The participants set their compasses (dial) so that the bearing on the compass housing is aligned with the direction of travel arrow. They turn about so that the magnetic needle (red) lies directly over the North arrow (striped). The participants will now be correctly oriented to travel on a bearing of 97°.
Repeat this activity several times using a variety of compass bearings. Remember to have the participant look at the feature or intended destination that they might travel toward.

e) Compass Bearing to a Feature
Have the participants choose a partner. Spread out in a "scatter formation" in the space available. One partner selects a feature and the other takes a compass bearing. Partner then tests the accuracy by checking the direction with his or her own compass. Give sufficient time to practise so both partners thoroughly understand the handling and use of the compass.

f) Concluding Activity
The Card Compass Game can be set up either in the gymnasium or on the playing field. The activity is designed to encourage more realistic use of the compass. See Indoor and Outdoor Compass Games, page 21.

4. Review

Briefly discuss purpose of the compass - that the compass gives direction.

Instructor's Note:

When teaching the compass avoid being near metallic objects; this may cause incorrect compass bearings.

Lesson Three

Objectives: To introduce map reading skills in navigation.
To appreciate the importance of orienting the map.

1. Introduction

a) Review function of the map - it gives a picture of the

ground.

b) Briefly recall the five characteristics of the map and the role of each.

2. Development

a) Distribute maps to class.

b) Present, through a simple demonstration on the chalkboard and with the use of maps, some of the basic navigation techniques:
   i) Use of trail - if it goes in general direction.
   ii) Use of open areas - field, easy traveling.
   iii) Use of large features - lake or hill because of easy identification on the map.

3. Activities

a) Locate the Basic Features on the map
   With a partner. Choose two locations and use the newly introduced techniques to travel between the locations with a verbal commentary.
   i) Suggest two obvious locations.
   ii) Allow participants to select their own features.

b) Orienting the Map
   Distribute a sheet which consists of four small pictures; under each there are four map drawings. Have the participants select the one map drawing that truly represents each of the four pictures.
   Keeping the map oriented at all times is an important factor in Orienteering, and this cannot be stressed enough.

c) Map Memory and Verbal Navigation Game
   See page 19.
   The purpose of the game is to describe a route between two features.

d) Map Symbol Relay (concluding activity) See page 18.
   The purpose of this activity is to test map symbol identification skills.

4. Review

Briefly discuss the importance of having the map oriented and of relating features to the map. These factors are the essence of sound map reading.

Lesson Four

Objectives: To review use of the compass.
            To introduce estimation of distance.

1. Introduction

a) Review how to use a compass to take accurate bearings.

b) Partner activity: select two features and determine exact starting location. Take compass bearings and compare results with partner.

2. Development

In Orienteering, pace counting is the technique used

to estimate distance.

a) Find an open space, preferably outdoors, and set up traffic cones 50 meters apart.

b) Line the participants beside the first cone and have them walk to the other cone counting the number of double strides it takes to travel the 50 meters. Two strides are equal to one Orienteering pace. When a number of paces has been determined by each participant, have the class jog, then run the same distance and count alternate strides. .

c) Repeat this activity once more for an accurate count. Record both their walking and jogging pace counts over the 50 meters.

3. Activities

a) Hunt the Silver Dollar   See page 20.
   This activity combines the use of the compass and pace counting.

b) Distance and Direction Orienteering (concluding activity)   See page 22.
   The purpose of this activity is to use the compass to give direction and pace counting to determine the distance.

Instructor's Note:

Each card control location should be able to be seen from the previous one, but the distance between card control locations should vary.

4. Review

Reiterate both the importance of accuracy in use of the compass to give directions and an estimation of distance determined by consistent pace counting.

Lesson Five

Objectives: To introduce the combined use of map and compass.
            Review pace counting.

1. Introduction

Review map reading, use of the compass and basic navigation in a brief class discussion.

2. Development

Introduce the method by which courses are printed on maps.

3. Activities

a) Taking the Bearing from the Map with the Compass
   Distribute blank maps and compasses. The blank map illustrates a course marked out with a series of circles, Start and Finish symbols and Magnetic North lines only. A line should link the Start triangle to the series of circles and the double circle Finish symbol.

Participants first orient their maps and take a bearing from the map with the compass in three stages:

i) Use the long edge of the compass; link the Start triangle to the first circle along the connecting line.

ii) Check that the North arrow points in the same direction as the arrow heads at the top of each meridian line, by turning the compass housing so that the North arrow (striped) is parallel to the meridian lines on the map.

iii) Read the bearing at the base of the direction of travel arrow on the compass. In order to know the exact direction in which to take the first step, remove the compass from the map. To get the map and compass oriented, turn around until the magnetic needle (red) is aligned over the North arrow (striped). The true direction of travel will be known.

b) Pace Counting Over 50 Meters

Set two traffic cones 50 meters apart and have participants review pace counting at three traveling speeds: walk, jog, run. Record the information and check their original calculations from previous session.

c) Miniature Orienteering (concluding activity)
See page 22.

The purpose of this activity is to reinforce, once again, how to determine distance and direction between known features.

4. Review

Briefly discuss the importance of accurate use of the compass (direction) and consistency in pace counting (distance).

Lesson Six

Objectives: Review of map reading skills.
Introduce some basic competitive procedures.

1. Introduction

Discussion of the following:

a) Start and Finish symbols are generally located in an open or semi-open area during an event.

b) Control flag is located on the feature in the center of the circle marked on the map.

c) Each control location is numbered and has an accompanying control description.

d) Connecting lines link the circles so that the participant follows the correct sequence of controls to complete the course.

2. Development

Review map reading skills through a brief discussion:

a) Feature - symbol recognition

b) Importance of being able to identify the exact location of a feature within a general setting of other features.

3. Activities

a) Map Memory Game   See page 19.
The purpose of this game is to reinforce map reading skills and to encourage recognition of the components of an Orienteering course.

b) Line Orienteering (concluding activity)
See page 23.
The purpose of this activity is to accurately locate card controls along a route and to record the information carefully by circling the precise location on the map.

Instructor's Note:

If time is short, then only one loop of the course need be completed since participants will return to the central starting location.

4. Review

Go over the importance of careful map reading and keeping the map oriented. Accuracy and knowing one's exact location at all times is very important.

Lesson Seven

Objectives: To introduce navigational techniques.
Review orienting the map.

1. Introduction

a) Use of trails.
b) Use of open areas.
c) Use of large features.

2. Development

a) Distribute maps and compasses.

b) Discuss and demonstrate basic navigational techniques.

i) Attack Point: A large feature that is between the participant and the control, which would assist in locating the control by reducing the distance between a known feature and the control.

ii) Aiming Off: When a compass bearing is deliberately taken so that the participant arrives to one side of the control. This is effective when the control is placed on a linear feature.

iii) Collecting Feature: A linear feature or large feature placed directly behind the control lcoation that will prevent the participant going too far if the control has been missed.

iv) Handrail: A large and easily identifiable feature that the participant can travel beside without too much reference to either map or compass.

3. Activity

"Do-It-Yourself" Orienteering   See page 23.
The purpose of this activity is to have participants a) realize the importance of *accurate* setting of the controls and b) to have maps oriented at all times during the activity.

Instructor's Note:

As a variation to this type of Orienteering the students may set their own course. Emphasize, a) participants must know exactly where they are going to place their controls before leaving the classroom, and b) on their return, time should be allowed for them to copy the entire course from the master map before the event begins.

Lesson Eight

Objective: Participation in Cross-Country Orienteering Event

1. Introduction

a) Brief review of basic map reading and compass skills.

b) Reinforce basic navigation techniques.

   Instructor's Note:

   The course should be set up ahead of class time with no more than sixteen controls, depending on whether it is arranged in a figure eight or clover leaf formation. Start and Finish are in the central location.

2. Development

a) Explanation of "competitive" procedures:
   i) Pre-marked map - course (and map case).
   ii) Control description sheet.
   iii) Score card and pen.
   iv) Time interval - independent navigation is desirable. However, participants may travel in pairs if necessary.
   v) Control flag and identification code on control.
   vi) Traveling quietly; minimum talking to others.
   vii) Start procedures - one minute to look at the map.
   viii) All must check in at end of course.

b) Review of basic navigational techniques. Discuss methods of getting re-oriented if participants are off course.

3. Activities

a) Cross-Country Orienteering Event   See page 24.
Purpose of the activity is to navigate around the course and to visit the correct controls in proper sequence and in the fastest possible time.
Participants are given a start time. Times are called out from a stop-watch. Whistle is blown to indicate starting times. Names are checked off on Start sheet. Each participant is given a map one minute before start time to become oriented. Compasses and pens should be used.

b) Concluding Activity
Encourage the participants to discuss their route selection and have them review the entire event with rest of the class.

4. Review

Briefly discuss the navigational techniques used and any difficulties encountered, for example, whether participants were able to jog or run the course.

Chapter Five
Evaluation

The uniqueness of Orienteering suggests that participants are constantly testing themselves as they experience the immediate impact of their own decisions. This situation may make any valid evaluation difficult to realize.

To obtain the most accurate assessment of psychomotor, cognitive and affective skills learned during an Orienteering unit, ideally every participant should be sent out alone to complete a cross-country Orienteering course through unknown terrain. However, since evaluation is considered a necessary part of any Physical Education program, the following procedures could be considered valid means of assessment.

It is suggested that evaluation should combine both theoretical and practical skills.

A. Evaluation of Participants

1. Theoretical Skills

A written quiz could be designed to test understanding in the following areas:
a) Historical development of the sport
b) Characteristics of maps
c) Mechanics of the compass
d) Principles of navigation
e) Competitive procedures

Sample Questions

A. General:

1. Describe the historical development of Orienteering from the early 1920s.
2. Describe an Orienteering activity.
3. Why is it necessary to develop a good level of fitness?
4. Describe the non-competitive style of the sport.
5. Describe the procedures followed at the start of an event.
6. Complete in one paragraph: "Since I started Orienteering ..."

B. Map:

1. What is the definition of a map?
2. What are characteristics of a map?
3. Where is Magnetic North located on a map?
4. What map characteristic denotes a change in elevation? Explain.
5. What is the purpose of the legend?
6. Explain how the scale is understood.

C. Compass:

1. What is the purpose of a compass?
2. Name the parts of the compass.
3. How is the compass oriented?
4. How is the compass held?
5. Describe the three-stage method of taking a compass bearing.

D. Navigation: (Many of these questions can be related to a simple black and white map.)

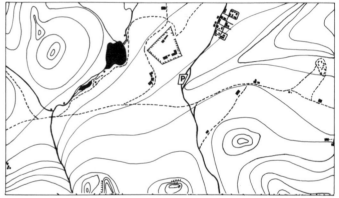

1. Define navigation.
2. In what way is independent navigation encouraged in Orienteering?
3. Describe on a map your route between two known features.
4. Calculate the distance that would be traveled between two known features if the direct route were taken.
5. Explain the fundamental guidelines for basic navigation.
6. Give the definition of the following navigational techniques:
   a) Attack Point   c) Collecting feature
   b) Aiming off   d) Handrail
7. From question six, identify and explain each technique on the map.

2. Practical Skills

Practical assessment could occur on the school campus or in a local park. It is suggested that the following areas be tested:
a) Sound map reading skills
b) Competent use of the compass
c) Accuracy in pace-counting to give an estimation of distance
d) Completion of a simple cross-country event in unknown terrain

e) Analysis of route choice

f) Improvement in general level of fitness

Sample Activities:

(Activities 1, 2 and 5 are described in Chapter Three.)

1. Identification of map symbols as demonstrated in the Map Symbol Relay.
2. Competent use of the compass, as demonstrated in Hunt the Silver Dollar.
3. Pace counting over selected distance. Convert paces into meters.
4. Accurately copy course from a Master map.
5. Combination of pace counting and use of compass in school yard compass game.
6. Completion of a cross-country event on an independent basis in unknown terrain and against the clock.
7. Design an illustrated quiz sheet that consists of the following activities:

   a) Identify symbols.

   b) Label compass parts.

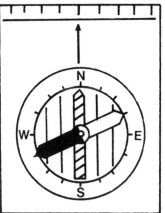

   c) Match contours with pictures.

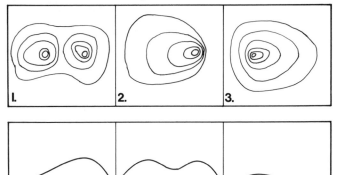

   d) Take compass bearings along a route drawn on the map.

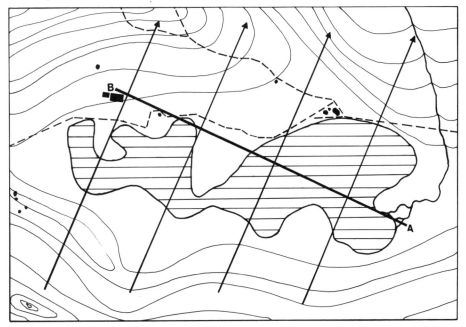

B. Program Evaluation

A successful Orienteering program is dependent upon many factors:

1. Knowledge and experience of the instructor
2. Instructor participation in an Orienteering event prior to teaching the unit
3. Attitude of participants to outdoor activity
4. Accessibility of a park close to the school
5. Weather and time of year
6. Participants who accept an opportunity to participate in a weekend event
7. Participants who have a good level of fitness
8. Participants who are willing to assist in map making, course setting, or meet organization

In summary, some participants will progress quickly through the levels, whereas others will need to review some of the basic skills before complete understanding is acquired. However, the essence of a successful program is that the participants had a meaningful and enjoyable experience in Orienteering.

Chapter Six
Making an Orienteering Map

Navigation is the basis of Orienteering and it is important to use an accurate map. A regular Orienteering map is a fairly large scale detailed topographical map of a hilly and forested area. The activity area selected must be large enough to accommodate the participants for about an hour as they complete their course.

Other maps may be used. Local street maps of the community surrounding the school can usually be obtained from the local municipal hall. Bicycle Orienteering has proved to be a most successful activity when using this type of map. See Chapter Three, page 24.

Topographical maps are readily available from most government offices and/or Parks Board offices. They generally provide additional information such as place names, but in many cases make use of an inappropriate scale which offers little assistance. However, for teaching purposes a simple sketch map is more than adequate in the initial stages of instruction.

If an Orienteering map of a suitable area close to the school does not exist, it may be necessary to draw one. This, of course, depends on the instructor's expertise and time. The map may be a simple sketch, a sophisticated fine color rendition or perhaps basic black and white. It is important to remember that without a map, Orienteering will lose most of its relevance as a worthwhile activity.

A. Sketch Map

A simple sketch map serves an important role if it accurately reflects a true picture of the ground or floor. The features should be drawn in proportion and maintain a consistent size. For ease of reproduction, draw the map in ink and keep the original copy so that alterations may be made later and the map re-used. With little time and minimal skill, a simple sketch can be reduced and used for basic map reading with the younger participants.

B. Black and White Map

Follow these seven simple steps:

1. Base Map:

A plan of the school buildings may be obtained from the school administration and can serve as the base map. When reduced, the plan and all relevant information should be able to fit comfortably on a 8½" x 11" sheet of paper.

2. Scale:

The size of the area determines the reduction of the base map. For example, the scale may be 1:1000, that is, one centimeter on the map is equal to 10 meters on the ground. Use pace counting to calculate the area that will be shown on the map.

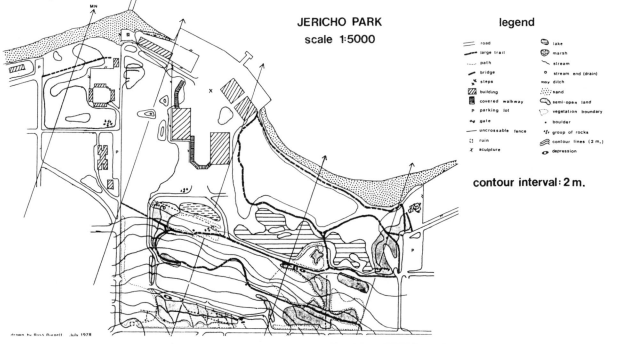

JERICHO PARK
scale 1:5000

legend

road		lake	
large trail		marsh	
path		stream	
bridge		stream end (drain)	
steps		ditch	
building		sand	
covered walkway		semi-open land	
parking lot		vegetation boundary	
gate		boulder	
uncrossable fence		group of rocks	
ruin		contour lines (2 m.)	
sculpture		depression	

contour interval: 2 m.

drawn by Ross Burnell   July 1978

3. Magnetic North:

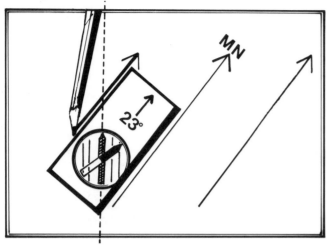

All Orienteering maps are drawn to Magnetic North. The base map will be drawn to True North. Magnetic declination varies. Set the compass accordingly. Align the North arrow with the edge of the base map and draw a line along the long edge of the compass. This line denotes Magnetic North. On the base map draw five meridian lines four centimeters apart and parallel to the original line. Write Magnetic North above these meridian lines at the top of the page. The map is now oriented to Magnetic North and can be used with the compass.

4. Field Work:

To be done well, field work takes time and perseverance. Basic equipment includes a clipboard; medium pencil(s); eraser; sandpaper; Silva compass; masking tape and a sheet of plastic tracing film. Tracing film is excellent to work with because pencil markings can be erased easily and it is waterproof. Keep the pencil sharp by using sandpaper that is adhered to the back of the clipboard. Place the sheet of tracing film over the base map and make a registration "cross" mark on both so that the information will be transposed correctly onto the final map.

First, walk around the outside of the area to obtain a general impression and to establish the boundaries of the area that is to be mapped. Carefully plot in all large features. The selection of small features depends on their relevance to the total picture of ground; unnecessary detail will clutter the map. Accuracy is very important in order that the relationship of one feature to another is truly represented in both distance and direction.

This can be accomplished in two ways:

a) Distance

Distance is measured by pacing. Two walking strides are equal to one Orienteering pace taken over a distance of 100 meters.

For example:

In 32 paces there are 50 meters. Therefore, in 48 paces there are 75 meters. If the distance between two features is 84 paces, this would be approximately 100 meters. Remember though because of differences in leg length, these distances are approximations.

b) Direction

Directions are determined by the use of the compass. The exact location of a feature can be found by taking a compass bearing from a known point. For example, take a bearing from the south wall of the gymnasium to the corner fence post behind the staff parking lot. This will give the true relationship between these two features. Next, find the same location on map and with the side of the compass, plot in the new feature at the correct distance and direction from the know feature. Repeat this procedure until all the required features have been recorded onto the base map.

5. Legend:

The legend provides a visual record of all features that are drawn on the map by making use of symbols as a means of identification. There is an international code of map symbols, but on school campus maps special features may be represented by unique symbols. Endeavor to keep the symbols fairly representative of the feature, even if this means inventing new symbols! Never draw any features on the map that are not described in the legend.

6. Drawing the Map:

This takes both time and a steady hand. Re-draw the map with a black ink fountain pen for better reproduction. Place a clean sheet of plastic tracing paper on top of the working copy and carefully transfer all the information from both the base map and field work. Letraset may be used for the title and legend. Scale is shown as Scale 1:1000 or the equivalent. Magnetic North is written at the top of the meridian lines.

7. Printing:

The final stage of the map. Black and white maps can be photocopied easily. Alternatively, ditto masters can be obtained in various colors so that a three-color map may be produced quite inexpensively.

C. Multi-Color Map

The same basic procedures should be followed in the production of a colored map as those suggested for the black and white map. However, for color printing, a carefully drafted sheet for each color must be produced in black. Normally, five colors are used on regular Orienteering maps.

Brown:	-contours and relief features
Black:	-man-made and rock features
Blue:	-water systems
Yellow:	-open areas
Green:	-vegetation features

A simpler, less refined color map can be made by using several ditto masters in different colors and then printing a three-color or four-color map.

Other factors influence the quality of any colored Orienteering map. Select an area that is small, close to home and not too detailed. Allow plenty of time for extensive field work so that there is, throughout the map, a consistency of feature representation, legibility of symbols and anything that is clearly visible on the ground. Good map making takes a great deal of time and effort.

If it is the intention to make a multi-color map, it would be advisable to contact the Provincial Orienteering Association for assistance.

Instructor's Note:

Orienteering maps are available in class sets from Provincial Orienteering Associations. See Appendix I.

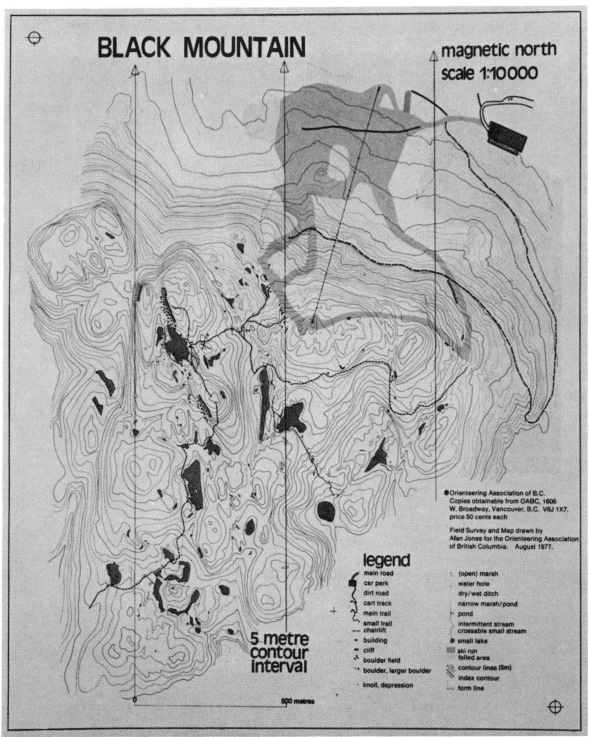

BLACK MOUNTAIN

magnetic north
scale 1:10 000

● Orienteering Association of B.C.
Copies obtainable from OABC, 1606
W. Broadway, Vancouver, B.C. V6J 1X7.
price 50 cents each

Field Survey and Map drawn by
Alan Jones for the Orienteering Association
of British Columbia.   August 1977.

legend

main road	(open) marsh
car park	water hole
dirt road	dry/wet ditch
cart track	narrow marsh/pond
main trail	pond
small trail	intermittent stream
chairlift	crossable small stream
building	small lake
cliff	ski run
boulder field	felled area
boulder, larger boulder	contour lines (5m)
knoll, depression	index contour
	form line

5 metre
contour
interval

0   500 metres

Chapter Seven
Setting An Orienteering Course

Although Orienteering is a competitive sport, this handbook has attempted to place emphasis on individual successes rather than on who is the best orienteer. The role of the course-setter then, is to ensure that all participants use their map reading and compass skills in fair competition and independent navigation.

Good course setting is dependent upon an accurate map. This map does not have to be sophisticated, but it must be a true reflection of the area it represents whether it be a school campus or local park.

As the basic navigational skills are learned, participants need to test their understanding in more challenging situations.

A. Course Setting for Simple Activities

It is best to begin with a simple map using the activities listed below.

1. Chalkboard Orienteering:

An easy course is set in a "scatter formation" by adhering small red stickers onto a variety of different objects with their location identified on the chalboard map. Thus an accurate map and a simple course, set in a familiar environment, can encourage a great deal of positive activity. See Chapter Three, page 20.

2. Score Orienteering:

The controls may be set out in a "scatter formation" as suggested in Chalkboard Orienteering. A variety of twenty control locations should be selected to challenge the skills of all participants. The use of directional information for the description of control locations may be appropriate, for example, fence, north east corner. Once again, it may be sensible to use small red stickers in a campus environment. See Chapter Three, page 23.

3. Distance and Direction Orienteering:

Make a set of red and white control cards that will provide directions in degrees and distances in meters. Next, using the gymnasium exit door as a starting point, design a course around the school campus. Use the compass to give the bearing to a prominent feature and pace count to that particular location. Record the information onto Start card and place by the gymnasium door. Identify the card by using a code letter or number. Continue this process making certain that each new feature (control location) is clearly visible from the previous location and that the distances between the controls vary. See Chapter Three, page 22.

4. Miniature Orienteering:

Fifteen feature locations are chosen in the gymnasium or on the playing field. To ensure that the course is a continuous one, it is essential to have the last feature location clearly visible from the first feature selected. It is best to walk or jog around the course prior to the event to determine the exact distances and directions between the control locations. See Chapter Three, Page 22.

B. Course Designs

These designs may vary according to the particular environment being used. The design used usually assists in the organization of the event:

1. Scatter formation   3. Figure eight
2. Star   4. Clover leaf

On each occasion, it is best to assess the area, the participant's experience and the level of activity and time available to accomplish the task.

C. Participants Set the Course

As participants gain confidence and experience in Orienteering, they should be encouraged to set the course as a class activity, for instance, "Do-It-Yourself" Orienteering (Chapter Three). Careful guidelines must be given and discussed prior to this task. Mistakes may be made, but any errors will be a learning experience. A familiar environment also helps make the event successful.

D. Guidelines for a School Event

Course setting is integral to any Orienteering activity and for novice participants in a park environment, it takes considerable care. The following general guidelines may be of assistance:

1. Number of Controls:

Initially, set the course on the map before visiting the park. Make sure that approximately ten features have been selected for possible control locations.

2. Control Locations:

These features should be trail bends and junctions; streams and path junctions; an edge of an open area; beside a lake or near any large identifiable feature.

3. Route Choice:

The location of these controls should be found by the use of linear features, for instance traveling on trails, following a stream or the use of the boundary of an open area.

4. Time Allowance:

Allow 20 to 45 minutes competition time. This depends on the number of participants and the start time allotted to them.

E. Reminders for Setting a Novice Course

1. Competition area includes:

a) A variety of features
b) A good network of trails
c) Large "collecting features", for example, lake, field, or fence

2. Start and Finish area:

Before setting out, participants must know where the Start and Finish areas are located on their maps.
a) Start and Finish areas are near the parking lot and washroom facilities.
b) Ideally, the Start should not be visible from the registration area.
c) Water containers should be available.

3. First control:

It is important to place the first control in a location which encourages participants to begin map reading immediately.

4. Control locations:

Controls are initially placed at nearby trail junctions, gradually extending the distance from the trail to large obvious features.

5. Route between controls:

Distance is relative, but initially there should be easy navigation between the controls. If possible, introduce one Orienteering problem at a time and gradually increase the difficulty as experience and confidence are developed.

6. Dog legs:

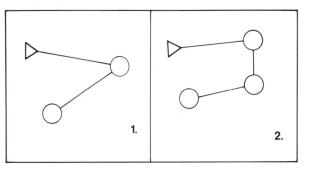

The angle of approach and departure to the control is too narrow and participants see each other. Avoid this situation.

7. Course layout:

Always have sufficient controls to present a reasonable challenge. Confidence in navigation skills will be developed as participants are guided along the trail system before going cross-country.

Instructor's Note:

Before the start of an event it would be a wise policy to have someone check out the course to eliminate any possibility of a misplaced control.

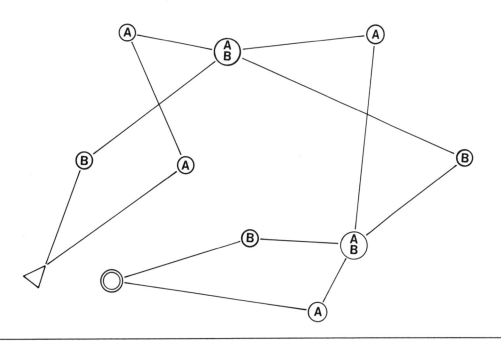

Chapter Eight
Organizing An Orienteering Meet

Orienteering can begin in the classroom and at this stage organization is simple. Remember, it is necessary to be adaptable whether organizing meets on the school campus or in the local park. Nothing can reinforce future participation in Orienteering like an initial enjoyable experience, so try to keep the organization simple and effective. A few guidelines as to the most logical and sensible way to organize a meet are recommended here.

It may be assumed that a map has been produced. This may be either a black and white map or a colored map printed by the Provincial Orienteering Association. A map is the basic piece of equipment, but control flags and punches (or pencils), score cards, a whistle, stop watch and compasses are necessary in organizing an event.

If the event is held in the local park, larger equipment would include table and chairs, portable chalkboard, streamers, water container and first aid box.

A. Equipment
1. Control flag:

Orange and white, the international colors of Orienteering, should be used in the production of a control. On the school campus small red stickers or small white cards with red felt pen markings are effective. In a more forested area or a park, a piece of stiff card painted half orange and white, slipped into a ziplock bag and hung by a length of string, is easily identified.

2. Control code:

Whatever the size or shape of the control being used, it should be identified by either a number or a letter. The purpose of a control code is that when the participants locate the control they will a) know where they are on the map and b) record the code on their score cards as a means of confirming that they have visited that particular control location. If regulation control flags and punches are used, the same procedures are followed but the participant punches the score card, leaving a unique imprint.

3. Score Cards:

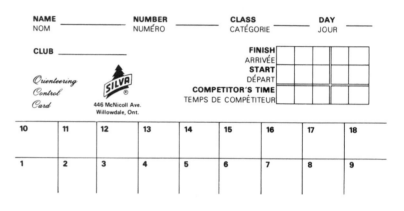

These may be the standard cards but any small card is acceptable providing that there is space available for name; class or group; recording of control punch or code, the start, finish and elapsed time.

4. The Whistle:

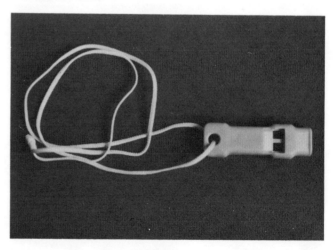

Encourages an element of control at the start of the event if not adding to the general air of anticipation!

5. Stop Watch:

It is always sensible to have two correctly functioning watches to record start times accurately. With a large number of participants (75-100), there is a possibility that early starters may be finishing before the last of the starters is underway. One stop watch should be taken to the Finish area.

6 Compasses:

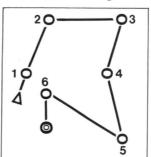

Initially it will not be necessary to use compasses, especially if map reading skills are being encouraged.

B. Pre-Meet Organization

The course(s) should be set, checked and printed on the maps prior to the event.

1. Master Maps:

If a map has not been produced prior to the meet, a master map may be used. Participants follow a marked trail from the Start area to the master map location and copy the course from the master map directly onto their maps.

2. Safety Bearing:

Should participants become disoriented, the safety bearing provides a method of relocation by using the compass on a specified bearing which will lead the participant to a major road or trail returning to the Start area. If safety bearings are used, print them on the map or on the control description sheet.

3. Control Description Sheet:

This may be a small sheet stapled to one corner of the map or printed onto the map itself. Information will include: control number; feature and directional information as appropriate, and the control code. Other information includes age/level of event; length of course; exact locations of Start and Finish areas. Have this information typed for clarity. Remind novice participants to check that the control code matches the information on their control description sheet.

4. Course Printing:

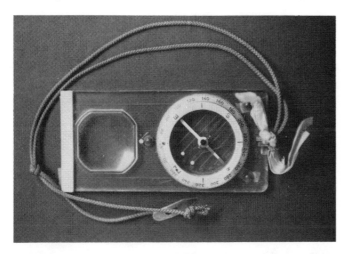

With red pen/pencil and template, mark maps with a triangle to identify the location of the Start area. Circle each feature ensuring that it is precisely in the center of the circle. Number every circle but do not obliterate any feature close to it as this may make navigation more difficult for the participants when they approach the control location.

The double circle represents the Finish area. On the control description sheet this symbol is accompanied by a brief statement giving the distance marked by streamers from the last control to the Finish.

5. Packaging:

If map cases or the equivalent are used, then control description sheets and named score cards for each participant may be stapled onto the back of the map at opposite corners so as not to block out important areas of the map. This prevents loss of either sheet or card - a frequent occurrence with novice participants.

6. Start Times:

Start times can be established ahead of the event if participants are known. Intervals between start times may vary from one to four minutes depending on the competition level. It is best to have a start time sheet and call participants to the starting line at least two minutes before they set off. The time interval between participants will hopefully allow for independent navigation, but to discourage "bunching-up" on the course, it is best for the instructor to group the participants.

C. Start Procedures

Two people can effectively coordinate the Start area. Participants must gather behind the start line. This can be the side-line of a soccer field or a length of rope placed on the ground in an open area of the local park. One person calls participants to the starting grid and checks their names off on the start times sheet. The second person serves as the Starter and calls out start times and blows the whistle to indicate when the participants may leave. It is helpful to have a large display clock showing the competition time.

Providing two minutes before start time allows participants to pick up pre-marked maps and control description sheets and gives them time for map examination. This encourages each participant to begin adjusting the relationship of the map to the terrain and then to navigate confidently to the first control.

The grid system is not necessary for a mass start. In Score Orienteering one person can coordinate the Start. Remember to record the start time accurately and to use a reliable clock to maintain the running time. Sometimes

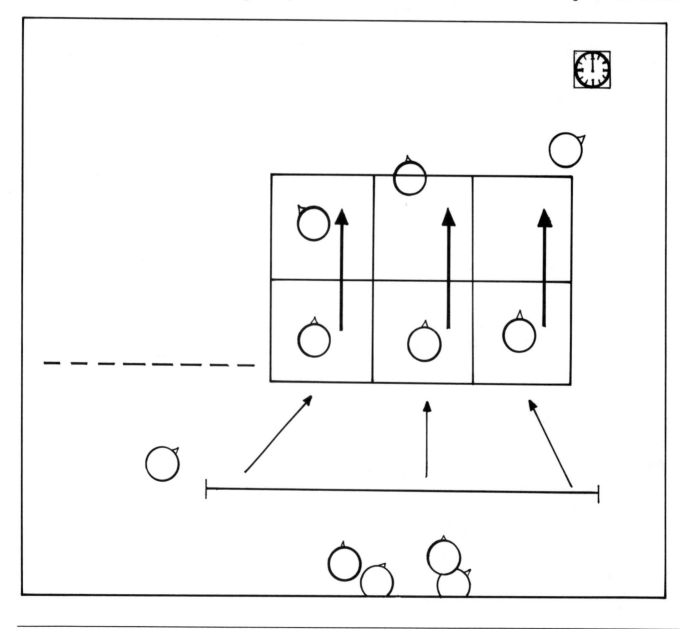

it helps to have maps posted on a board so participants may become familiar with the area through general map reading.

D. Finish Procedures

A funnel or chute is used at the Finish. This roped-off area allows individuals to be channeled across the finish line so times may be recorded accurately.

It is ideal to have three or four people assisting at the Finish but, with the help of non-participants, the two people officiating at the Start can handle the situation efficiently. Their most important function is to record the time accurately and to assign the correct time to the right participant.

An assistant can collect the score cards in the correct sequence while another posts the results. This allows two people to call out finish times and record each time onto the appropriate card.

The timer stands at the finish line near the recorder. Finish times are recorded on a time sheet and then transformed, in correct sequence, to each of the participants' score cards.

To calculate time elapse, subtract start time from finish time and post the results in minutes and seconds.

Always allow time at the end of the event for participants to discuss the routes they selected. This review can reinforce a great many of the skills introduced over the previous weeks. However small the

event, it may be appropriate to present ribbons, or equivalent, to all participants.

Participation in an event sponsored by a Provincial Orienteering Association or local club would be an ideal way to introduce young participants to a more competitive situation in which the teacher does not have the responsibility of meet organization.

Conclusion
Integration Of Orienteering Into The Curriculum

Orienteering is an activity that could be considered from a variety of starting points, only one of which would be Physical Education. It might best be taught through implementation of an integrated program with several departments, for instance, Science, Math and Social Studies, coordinated by Physical Educators. In Math there could be a useful discussion on measurement, estimation of distance and the appreciation of scale. To accompany this understanding, the use of magnets, compasses and awareness of the environment could be easily incorporated into the Science program.

Other Orienteering skills such as maps and map reading could be introduced into the Geography content of the Social Studies curriculum.

The "unseen" curriculum which deals with developing responsibility, perseverance and organizational activities should not be ignored.[1] Since the nature of Orienteering is to motivate individuals to develop decision-making powers in a non-structured environment, any reinforcement from other areas of school curricula should be encouraged in presenting theoretical aspects before practical application.

It should not be forgotten that substantial planning is needed to present a successful Orienteering program. Perhaps if a team teaching/interdepartmental approach could be taken, effective use of several teachers' skills would enhance the program. At the same time, it may provide the students with lasting appreciation and respect for the environment as well as an ability to travel through it with skill and safety. It is hoped that Orienteering might be of lifetime value to its participants.

[1]Parry, John. *Orienteering as the Basis for an Integrated Curriculum in the Elementary School,* B.C.T.F. Lesson Aids. 1976.

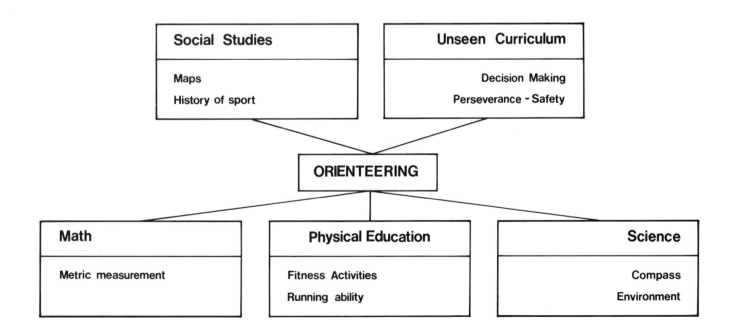

Appendix I
Reference Materials

A. Books

1. Teaching

a) Andresen, Steve. *The Orienteering Book.* California: World Publications, 1977.

b) Anthony, A. *Orienteering is Fun - Teaching and Resource Package.* Vancouver, B.C.: British Columbia Teacher's Federation, Lesson Aids Service, 1977.

c) Bengtssow, H. and Atkinson, G. *Orienteering for Sport and Pleasure.* Vermont: Stephen Greene Press, 1977

d) Berglund, Berndt. *The Complete Guide to Orienteering in North America.* Pagurian Press Ltd., 1979.

e) Canadian Orienteering Services. *Teaching Orienteering Using the Direct Method.* Willowdale, Ont.: 1976.

f) Disley, J. *Orienteering. Stackpole: Thomas Nelson,* 1973.

g) *Your Way with Map and Compass.* Willowdale, Ont.: Canadian Orienteering Service, 1975.

h) Gilchrist, J. *Teaching Orienteering.* Willowdale, Ont.: Canadian Orienteering Service, 1975.

i) Harris, Norman. *Orienteering for Fitness and Pleasure.* Surrey, U.K.: World Work Ltd. Windmill Press, 1978.

j) Kjellstrom, B. *Be Expert with Map and Compass.* New York: Charles Scribner & Sons, 1976.

k) Know the Game Series, *Orienteering.* Yorkshire: E.P. Publishing Ltd., 1965.

l) Know the Game Series, *Orienteering. Yorkshire: E.P. Publishing,* 1976.

m) Palmer, P. *Orienteering for the Young.* England: Warrick Printing Co., Ltd., 1976.

2. Map Making

a) Gilchrist, J. *Preparing a Simple Orienteering Map.* Willowdale, Ont.: Canadian Orienteering Services, 1974.

b) Harvey, R. *Map Making for Orienteers.* Lea Green, Nr. Matlock, U.K.: British Orienteering Federation, 1976.

c) Outdoor Education Manual, No. 7. *Drawing a Contour Map.* Maple Ridge: U.B.C. Research Forest, 1974.

3. Course Setting

a) Harvey, Sue (translator). *Course Planning.* Nr. Matlock, Derbyshire U.K.: British Orienteering Federation.

4. Meet Organization

a) Gilchrist, J. *Organizing and Running a Simple Orienteering Meet.* Willowdale, Ont.: Canadian Orienteering Services, 1976.

b) Ontario Orienteering Association. *Organizing an Orienteering Meet.* Toronto, Ont., 1974.

Available from Canadian Orienteering Services, (Silva Ltd.), 446 McNicholl Avenue, Willowdale, Ontario. M2H 2E1 (416) 499-1988.

B. Audio Visual

1. Films

a) "What Makes Them Run," Recreation and Fitness Branch Film Library, 800 Hornby Street, Vancouver, B.C. 688-2732; or National Film Board, 1161 Georgia Street, Vancouver, B.C. 666-1716.

*b) "Thomas the Orienteer"

*c) "Orienteering, Family Fun and Fitness"

*d) "Orienteering"

*e) "By Map and Compass"

*f) "Navigation in the Hills"

*g) "Invisible Force of Direction"

*Available from: Canadian Orienteering Services, (Silva Ltd.), 446 McNicholl Avenue, Willowdale, Ontario. M2H 2E1 (416) 499-1988.

h) Three-part teaching film on Orienteering, Map and Compass. (Three ten-minute Super 8 sound movies) produced by Anne Anthony. Available from Resource Centre, British Columbia Teachers' Federation, 2235 Burrard Street, Vancouver, B.C. V6J 3H9 731-8121.

C. Orienteering Maps

1. All Orienteering maps suitable for school or community use are available from Provincial/State

Orienteering Assocations.

2. Legend for Orienteering Maps

Road
Trail
Small footpath
Railway
Stream
Fence
Building
Ruin

Boulder
Contours
Depressions
Cliff
Knoll
Open area
Vegetation boundary
Any other object (must be explained)

D. National and Provincial Orienteering Associations

Canadian Orienteering Federation
333 River Road
Vanier City, Ontario
K1L 8B9 (613) 741-9427

Federation Canadianne de Course Orientation
333 River Road
Vanier City, Ontario
K1L 8B9

Orienteering Association of British Columbia
c/o Sport B.C.
1200 Hornby Street
Vancouver, B.C.
V6Z 1W2 (604) 687-3333

Alberta Orienteering Association
P.O. Box 88
Calgary, Alberta

Saskatchewan Orienteering Association
c/o Saskatchewan Culture and Youth
Avord Towers, 11th Floor
Regina, Saskatchewan
S4P OR7

Manitoba Orienteering Association
c/o Sport Administration Centre
1301 Ellice Avenue
Winnipeg, Manitoba

Orienteering Ontario
c/o Sport Ontario
559 Jarvis Street
Toronto, Ontario

Orienteering Quebec
1415 Jarry Street East
Montreal, Quebec
H2E 2Z7

Federation Quebecoise
de Course d'Orientation
1415 est rue Jarry
Montreal, Quebec
H2E 2Z7

Orienteering New Brunswick
c/o New Brunswick Sport Federation
43 Brunswick Street
Fredericton, N.B.
E3B 1G5

Orienteering Association of Nova Scotia
P.O. Box 3010 South
Halifax, Nova Scotia.

Newfoundland Orienteering Association
c/o Newfound Labrador Amateur
Sport Federation
Box 1597
St. John's, Newfoundland

Residents of Prince Edward Island, Yukon, North West Territories, please contact the national office.

For further information in the U.S.A., please contact:

Orienteering Services U.S.A.
Box 547, La Porta, Indiana 46350
U.S.A.

E. Control Descriptions

Symbol		Symbol	
Knoll	Ditch		
Hill	Marsh		
Spur	Field		
Re-entrant	Meadow		
Depression	Vegetation-boundary		
Cliff	Clearing		
Pit	Path		
Bare rock	Road		
Lake	Bridge		
Pond	Fence		
Stream	Building		
Boulder	Ruin		

F. TRIM Orienteering

A permanent course established in a park is called TRIM Orienteering. This permanency refers to the controls which are either specifically marked trees or a series of short posts set in the ground. There are at least 15 to 20 of these permanent controls in the area depending upon the size and suitability of the park. Information packages should be readily available close to the park area and should contain:

pre-marked map	score card
control description sheet	instruction sheet
ziplock bag	contact information

TRIM is a form of "do-it-yourself" Orienteering. There is no competitive element in this activity, since everyone goes at his or her own pace. All control locations can be visited in at least half a day.

This form of Orienteering is ideal for school programs, clubs, training sessions and family groups. The first permanent course was established in Vancouver's Stanley Park in 1977 and teachers throughout the Lower Mainland area are able to purchase multi-packages for school use. On successful completion of any of the five courses, TRIM badges are awarded to participants through the Orienteering Association of British Columbia.

TRIM Orienteering gives participants the opportunity to travel independently in the park and to enjoy the challenge of map reading in order to locate controls. As with all forms of Orienteering, TRIM can be a lifetime pursuit for those seeking some form of physical activity and mental stimulation.

Contact Provincial or State Orienteering Associations for information concerning local TRIM courses.

"Spot the post" a family goes orienteering in the park.

Appendix II
Historical Background

Orienteering is thought to have evolved from Swedish military training in the late nineteenth century and it became established as a competitive sport in the early twenties. Major Ernst Killander held the first meet outside Stockholm in which there were 220 participants. Since then, Orienteering has become the national sport of Sweden as well as a mandatory part of the school curriculum. It has been described as "self chosen route in unknown terrain, clear thoughts during physical strain, quick decision in tough competition."

The sport spread quickly throughout the Scandinavian countries and the definition used by the Danish Orienteering Federation is "to complete a course consisting of a series of control locations set in the terrain and marked on the competitor's map, in as short a time as possible. The terrain should be natural as possible and be unknown to the competitors."

The growth of Orienteering was dependent upon two major factors: the invention of the simple one-piece protractor compass by the Kjellström brothers and the production of highly detailed and accurate maps. These improvements in basic equipment enabled the sport to spread rapidly throughout Europe. Bjorn Kjellström introduced Orienteering to North America in the forties and anglicized the Swedish term "the sport of Orientation"; Orienteering now is an international word.

The late Professor Alex "Sass" Peepre of University of Guelph was mainly responsible for gaining both recognition and financial support for Orienteering from the Canadian Government in the mid-sixties.

In 1967 Peepre became the founding President of the Canadian Orienteering Federation and in the following year the first national championships were held in Ottawa with 116 participants.

The sport has spread across Canada and Provincial Associations support 60 clubs and a membership of approximately 2,000 orienteers.

In 1975 the first national Leadership Development clinic sponsored by Recreation Canada was held at the University of Guelph. As a result of this clinic, the four West Coast delegates established the Orienteering Association of British Columbia at a conference held at the University of British Columbia two months later.

In 1976 Canada was the first country outside Europe to host a five-day international event called Quebec O'Ring. It was the largest Orienteering event in North America with 1,200 participants. However, at a larger international event in Europe as many as 14,000 participants will be competing.

Orienteering is a truly international sport and has gained Olympic status. The International Orienteering Federation (I.O.F.) now represents 26 national bodies and the sport continues to grow throughout the world.

Appendix III
Glossary

Aiming Off: A compass bearing taken so that the participant arrives to one side of the control.

Attack Point: A large feature that is located between the participant and the control, hence reducing the margin of error in locating the control.

Collecting Feature: Generally a linear feature located directly behind the control that prevents the participant from going too far past the control location.

Compass Bearing: Gives the direction of travel.

Contours: Lines drawn on the map joining points of the same elevation. Lines close together denote steepness; those widely spaced denote a gradual slope.

Control Card: A card marked in some way as evidence that the participant has located each control.

Control Code: Numbers or letters which identify each control flag.

Control Description: A sheet attached to the map that gives information about features (control locations) to be found during the event.

Control Flag: An orange and white tubular flag that identifies a control location.

Control Punch: Orange stapler that leaves a distinctive imprint on the control card.

Handrail: A large feature such as a lake, that the participant can easily run beside without constant reference to map or compass.

Map Reading By Thumb: A simple but important technique. The participant's location is identified by placing the thumb on the map to mark the last exact known location. The thumb is moved to different places on the map as the participant travels the route.

Map Scale: The ratio of distance on the map to the distance on the ground.

Master Map: A map on which the course is printed. Participants copy the course on their own maps from the Master Map.

Orienting The Map: The map should always be oriented to North by matching Magnetic North (lines) on the map to the direction of Magnetic North on the ground (by use of compass). The direction of travel is then determined correctly.

Pace Counting: A technique used to estimate distance. Two walking strides are equal to one Orienteering pace.

Pre-Marked Maps: A map on which the course has been printed prior to the start of the event.

Rough Compass: Running quickly on an approximate bearing, usually to a collecting feature.

Route Choice: A choice of route that allows the participant to make the best use of the terrain and still maintain a reasonable speed.

Safety Bearing: A bearing, for example 33°, that provides a method of relocation by using the compass on a specified bearing which will lead the participant to a major road or trail returning to the Start area.